exciting ways to make
presents

about this book

This do-it-yourself craft book has been specially designed for children. It has step-by-step pictures and words so that you can work without adult help.

This book is all about making presents. Many of them can be made from ordinary things such as old bottles and jars, toilet-roll tubes and crêpe paper, parcel string and scraps of felt. Some presents would be best for a mum or dad, but there are others you can give to brothers, sisters and friends. There are so many super presents to make that you will probably want to keep at least one for yourself! There are also lots of ideas for wrapping presents so that they look exciting.

The chapters are arranged according to the materials used. Within each chapter the easier projects come first and the more difficult ones follow.

The blue tag at the side of a page tells you the material used in that chapter. All the projects between one tag and another use the same or a similar material.

The 'Try it first' tag at the top of a page indicates a practice section. This gives you the chance to try out a simple project before starting on a bigger, more exciting one.

Before you start, it's helpful to read the 'Useful Things to Know' pages overleaf.

Useful things to know

Before you begin making a present, look through the whole project first. This will give you a good idea of what you are going to do.

Try to clear as much space to work in as possible. If your project involves messy things like paint, dye or glue, cover working areas with newspaper. And wear an apron or an old shirt over your clothes.

When you finish, wrap up the rubbish in a newspaper and throw it away. Save scraps of cloth, rope and other materials so that you can use them to make more things later. Put the lids back on tins and tubes. Clean up your work surface and equipment you have used.

Paints and dyes

You can buy most kinds of paint in a do-it-yourself or hardware shop.

Enamel is a shiny paint. You need to shake the tin and stir the paint before using it. It takes about six hours to dry.

Primer is a sealing paint. Put it on bare wood first to stop the wood soaking up your top coat of enamel. Leave primer for six hours to dry.

Fabric dyes are used to print colourful designs on cloth. Use Rowney's fabric dye or Dylon Color-fun fabric paint. Fix the colours to the cloth by ironing it on the wrong side when the paint is dry.

Rope

There are many kinds of rope, string and cord.

Hemp and sisal are ropes made from natural fibres. They come in varying thicknesses and are a natural 'string' colour.

Synthetic ropes come in many colours and thicknesses. Nylon rope is one kind, but some synthetic ropes have odd names like Polypropylene.

Using trace patterns

All the trace patterns in this book are printed the right way round.

To trace a pattern, you will need tracing paper, a soft pencil (such as a 2B) and paper clips. You could use airmail paper or waxed kitchen paper for tracing.

1. Lay the tracing paper over the pattern and fix it to the page with paper clips. Draw round the outline.

2. Cut out the shape.

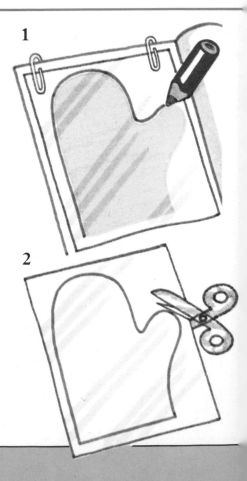

1

2

Paintbrushes

Water-colour brushes are ideal for painting small areas.
To paint bigger areas, you will need a paintbrush about 1cm wide. Do-it-yourself and hardware shops sell these.
If you paint with enamel or primer, clean your brushes in white spirit.

Glue and tape

Clear glue is best for sticking heavy things. Bostik 1 and UHU are both clear glues.
Fabric glue such as Copydex is ideal for sticking pieces of cloth and felt.
Double-sided sticky tape is sticky on one side and has a paper backing on the other.
Put the sticky side down.
Peel off the paper and press another surface to the tape.

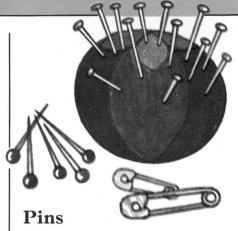

Pins

For most projects, ordinary straight pins are used.
Glass-headed pins are longer and have glass knobs on the ends. They are used for pinning heavy materials such as string and rope.
Safety-pins are the ones that can be closed.

1
2

Drawing a square

Rule a straight line to the measurement you need. Put a protractor on the line, with its centre at the end of the line.
1. Find 90° and mark it.
2. Rule a line through the mark to the first line, making it the same length.
Use the protractor in the same way to draw the third side.
Join up the last side.

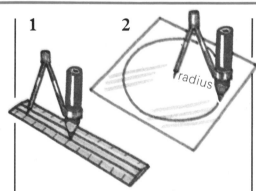

1　　　　2

radius

Drawing a circle

1. Set the arms of a pair of compasses against a ruler, and measure the distance of the radius of the circle you want. Put the pin arm on the paper or cardboard to mark the centre of the circle.
2. Swing the pencil arm round to draw a complete circle.

TAKE CARE!

An important part of making things is learning to use tools and materials properly.
Scissors should be kept closed when not in use. Work with the tips facing away from your body.
Pins and needles are best kept in a pincushion. Never leave them lying about.
Knives should never be used with the sharp side of the blade facing you. Keep your fingers well away from the blade when you cut things.
Compasses have sharp points. Always cork or tape the point when not using the compasses.
Other people's things must be respected. Always ask before you use something that doesn't belong to you.
Now have fun and be safe, too!

Bottles and jars

Don't throw away old bottles and jars! Turn them into exciting presents by painting them with bright colours. Make the glass containers into special storage jars, beautiful vases or candle-holders.

▶ You will need:
- ☐ Glass bottles and jars
- ☐ Enamel paint, paintbrushes
- ☐ White spirit, clean cloth
- ☐ Newspapers
- ☐ Gummed paper shapes (optional)

Painting the outside

Spread lots of newspaper over your work surface.
1. Rinse out all the containers with white spirit, and wipe the outside of each one with a cloth dipped in the spirit.
You need to do this before you paint any glass container.
Let the containers dry.

2. Dip a thick brush in paint. Don't use too much paint.
3. Use long strokes to spread the paint evenly over the surface of the bottle or jar. Hold the container at the top and turn it as you paint.
Paint the top last.
Let the paint dry overnight.

Painting the inside

1. Pour some paint into the bottle or jar.
Put the lid on the container.
2. Tilt the container to swirl the paint about until the inside surface is evenly coated.
Pour out the extra paint and leave the container to dry.

Marbling the inside

Pour a tiny bit of paint into the jar. Tilt the jar gently and turn it a few times to get a streaky effect.
When the paint is dry, do the same with another colour.
Or put the lid on the container and shake up the paint to make a pattern.

Making patterns

1. Stick gummed shapes on the glass before painting the outside.
2. When the paint is dry, peel off the shapes so that the glass can be seen.
Or simply stick shapes or letters on your painted glass.
Or paint birds, trees and flowers freehand, if you like.

Buy the basic materials from a do-it-yourself shop. Primer comes in white, grey and pink—use whichever you like. Clean up with white spirit and wash your brushes in it later.

Tool tidy board

This is made in almost exactly the same way as the kitchen tidy, but it is a larger project and you may need to do it in several stages. Ask mum to help keep your plan secret!

Gather together dad's tools.
1. Lay the pegboard down and arrange the tools on it.
2. Fix the tools into place with the hooks and clips.
Stand the pegboard upright.
Now repeat steps 4-6 of the 'Try it first' project.
You could apply two coats of varnish to the pegboard to make the paint last longer.

Tidy boards

With a little patience (and a steady hand), you can make very useful presents by painting outlines on a board. First, try making a kitchen tidy. Then, you could paint the large tidy board for dad's tools. Ask an adult's permission before you start either project!

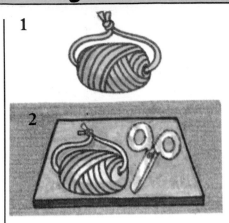

Kitchen tidy board

1. Cut off a piece of string.
Thread it through the centre of
the ball and knot the ends.
Lay the wood flat.
2. Arrange the scissors and ball
of string on the board.
Try to balance the shapes so
that they look attractive.

3. Position two cup-hooks and
screw them into place.
Hang the scissors and ball of
string on the cup-hooks.
Stand the wood upright.
4. Draw the outlines of the
scissors and ball of string.
Remove the objects and the
cup-hooks.

5. Fill in the shapes with
primer.
Let the primer dry.
6. Paint over the primer with
one coat of enamel paint.
Let the paint dry, and then put
on a second coat of enamel.
When the enamel is dry, you
could varnish the whole board.

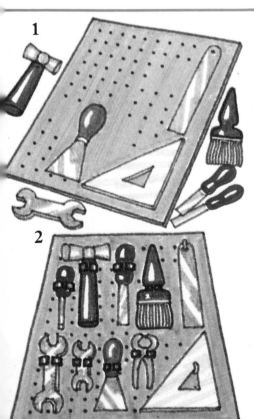

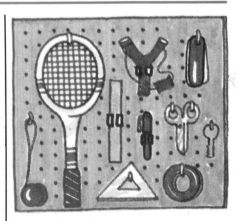

Hanging the boards

For the kitchen tidy, screw two
cup-hooks into the back of the
board.
Tie a length of string round
the hooks so that the board can
be hung on a nail.
The tool tidy can be nailed to a
frame. It would be best to let
dad decide where he wants to
put the board.

Other ideas

Tidy boards are useful for lots
of things. Paint shapes on a
board for hanging up tennis
racquets, toys and all kinds of
odds and ends.
Or ask an adult if you could
use the same idea on shelves or
in broom cupboards.

Fun with transfers

Transfer decorations can make ordinary objects look special in just a few minutes. Start by putting transfers on old glass or plastic containers. A jar decorated with flowers looks lovely with coloured bath salts or cotton wool in it. Or you could put animal transfers on a container for baby's safety pins.

Later, you could plan transfer decorations for tin mugs or wooden boxes. Transfers are so easy to use you may not be able to stop thinking up new ways to make super presents with them!

Beautiful jars

▶ You will need:
- ☐ Glass or plastic containers
- ☐ Water transfers
- ☐ Small bowl of warm water
- ☐ Large bowl of soapy water
- ☐ Scissors
- ☐ A clean, soft cloth
- ☐ Nail polish remover and a cloth
- ☐ Newspaper
- ☐ Clear varnish and a brush (optional)

If you spill nail polish remover, it will damage wooden or painted surfaces. make sure your working area is covered with lots of newspaper and mop up any spills immediately.

1. Soak the containers in soapy water to clean them and to remove paper labels.
2. Wipe the outside of the containers with a cloth dipped in nail polish remover.
This will erase brand names printed on plastic and remove any old glue.

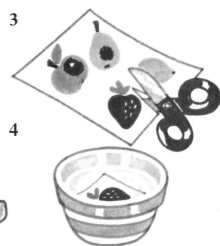

Transfers usually come on sheets of backing paper.
3. Cut out the transfers you want to use.
4. Soak one at a time in warm water until the transfer begins to come away from the paper. This will take a few seconds.

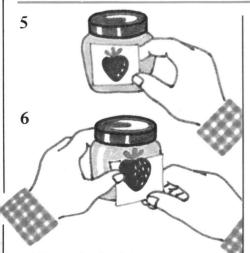

5. Place the backing paper against the container.
6. Hold the transfer gently with one hand and slide the backing paper down and away.
Slide the transfer round while it is still wet if you need to position it.

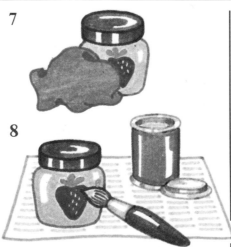

7. Wipe off excess water and push out any air bubbles by smoothing the transfer gently with the clean, soft cloth. Leave the transfer to dry.
8. If you varnish the container your transfer will last longer. *Do not eat or drink from varnished containers, or put food in them.*

Bright tin mugs

Shiny tin mugs can be decorated in exactly the same way as the glass and plastic containers.
You will need tin mugs instead of containers, and all the other 'Try it first' things except nail polish remover and a cloth.
You could make mugs for all the family. Put on a different design for each person or use transfer initials.
Remember that you must not use varnish if they are meant to be drinking mugs.
Or decorate mugs for holding pencils, paints or dried flowers. Some of your friends might like boldly-decorated mugs to brighten up their shelves or cupboards.

Cheerful clowns

These happy clowns are sharing a secret—each one is hiding a tube full of sweets! You could make one as a present for a special friend. Or decorate a party table with many clowns.

▶ You will need:
- ☐ Toilet-roll tube, sweets
- ☐ White crêpe paper
- ☐ Coloured crêpe paper
- ☐ Shiny cardboard
- ☐ White paper, scissors, pair of compasses, pencil
- ☐ Shiny sticky tape, ruler
- ☐ Gummed paper shapes
- ☐ Button thread, clear glue

Making the body

You can make two clowns from one toilet-roll tube.
1. Cut the tube in half.
Cut the white crêpe paper 20cm square.
2. Wrap the white crêpe paper round one half of the tube.
3. Tie one of the ends of the crêpe paper with button thread.

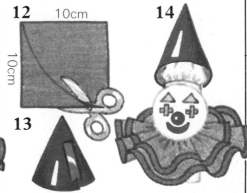

4. Fill the tube with sweets.
5. Tie the other end of the crêpe paper to close the tube.
Cut the coloured crêpe paper 20cm by 60cm.
Cut the white paper into a circle with a radius of 2·5cm.
(Look at the 'Useful things to Know' pages to help you.)

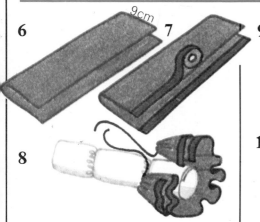

Putting on the frills

6. Fold the coloured crêpe paper over 9cm, long edges parallel.
7. Stick shiny sticky tape on both long edges.
Slip a long piece of button thread under the fold.
8. Gather the paper along the thread, and tie the frill tightly round one end of the tube.

Decorating the face

9. Cut and stick the gummed paper shapes to the circle of white paper to make a face. Stand the tube up on its frill.
10. Put a dot of glue on the back of the paper circle.
11. Glue the face to the tube just above the top of the frill.

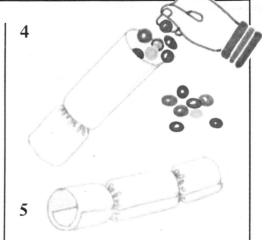

Making a hat

Cut the cardboard 10cm square.
12. Draw a curve on the square of shiny cardboard as shown. Cut along the curved line.
13. Make the edges of the cone meet and overlap slightly. Put sticky tape along the join.
14. Put the cone over the crêpe paper top.

11

Trendy canvas shoes

Fabric dye is very easy to use. You draw shapes on cloth and simply fill in the outlines with dye. Jazz up a friend's old tennis shoes or sneakers by dyeing bright patterns on them. (First ask your friend's mum if she thinks this is a good idea.) You can also make dye designs on T-shirts, denim jackets and jeans, or canvas hats and bags. Designing a pattern on shoes needs some patient planning. Try dyeing a cloth picture first. If you splash fabric dye on your clothes, wash it out with water immediately. And wash brushes in water before the dye makes them hard. Paintbrushes with stiff bristles are the easiest to use.

1

A sunny picture

First practise painting an easy design for a cloth picture.

▶ You will need:
☐ Square of canvas or cotton
☐ Fabric dyes, paintbrushes
☐ Pencil, ruler, scissors
☐ Fabric glue and cardboard

1. Draw a sun on the cloth.

2

Dip your paintbrush in dye. Don't overload the brush or you will get a blob of colour. Carefully fill in part of the design with one colour. Let this first colour dry.
2. Finish painting the design with different colours. Let each colour dry before you add another one.

3

Cut a piece of cardboard 2cm smaller than the cloth. Make sure the cloth is dry. Then put it face down with the cardboard on top of it.
3. Smear glue along the edges on the back of the cloth, and press them on to the cardboard.

1

Stylish walkers

You need a very steady hand!

▶ You will also need:
☐ Old canvas shoes, pencil
☐ Soapy water, scrubbing brush
☐ Fabric dyes, paintbrushes
☐ New pair of shoe-laces

1. Remove the old laces and give the shoes a good scrub.

Make sure the shoes are completely dry. Study the shape and style of the shoes carefully, and plan your design to suit them. For instance, little flowers and dots look good drawn round the holes for laces. You can also use the lines of stitching as a guide for your pattern.
2. Lightly draw your design. Put a little dye on the brush.
3. Fill in the outlines with one colour at a time as shown in 'Try it first'.
4. When the shoes are dry, thread them with new laces.

2

3

4

trace patterns

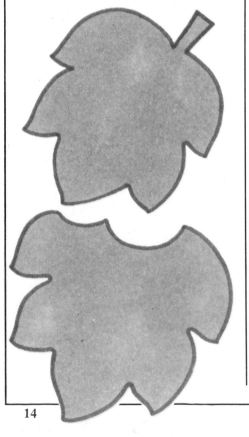

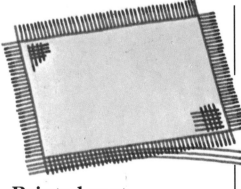

Printed mat

▶ You will need:
- ☐ All the 'Try it first' things except the napkin
- ☐ Piece of white linen or cotton, 27 cm × 40cm
- ☐ Carrots, kitchen knife
- ☐ Scissors, ruler

Make a fringe by pulling out an even number of threads from each side of the mat.

Making a pattern

Cut the tracing paper the same size as your mat.
Sketch a basket on the paper. Copy the shape of the one in the photograph.
1. Trace the leaves from the two patterns on to the paper. You can position the leaves anywhere you like because it's easy to fill in with grapes.
2. Draw over the basic outline with the felt-tipped pen.
3. Put the paper pattern under the mat and lightly chalk the outline on to the cloth. Remove the pattern.
Chop the carrots into triangles, diamonds and straight sticks.

14

Printed table mat

Printing with fabric dye is great fun. The simplest printing is done with your finger, but you can print lots of other shapes with carrots. Or fill in traced outlines with dye. A printed table mat would make a lovely present for gran or an aunty. Look at pages 12-13 for some more ideas. Always ask first if you plan to use things that belong to someone else.

Remember to wash dye off your clothes and brushes with water.

Printed napkin

► You will need:
☐ White linen or cotton napkin
☐ Fabric dyes, paintbrushes
☐ Coloured dressmaker's chalk
☐ Black felt-tipped pen
☐ Tracing paper, pencil and paper clips

Trace a pattern for the stalked leaf. (Look at the 'Useful things to know' pages to help you.)
Outline the drawing with the black felt-tipped pen.
1. Put the tracing paper under the napkin and lightly chalk a leaf outline on the cloth. Remove the pattern.
2. Fill in the outline with dye.
3. Dip your finger in dye and make fingerprints for grapes.

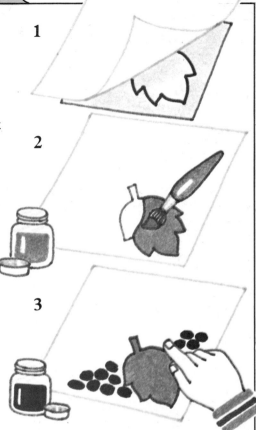

Printing the design

Brush dye quite thickly on a triangle of carrot.
1. Make the bottom row of the basket by pressing the painted triangle on to the mat.
Make sure you work within the chalked outline.
Print the basket by dyeing the other carrot shapes and pressing them on the mat.
Fill in the leaf shapes as shown for the napkin.
2. To get a variety of shapes, simply fill in part of some of the leaves with dye.
(Rub off the chalk marks when the colour is dry.)
3. Print the grapes as shown in step 3 of 'Try it first'.
Iron the mat on the wrong side to fix the colours. Ask an adult which temperature to use .

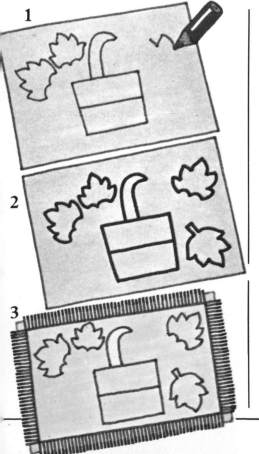

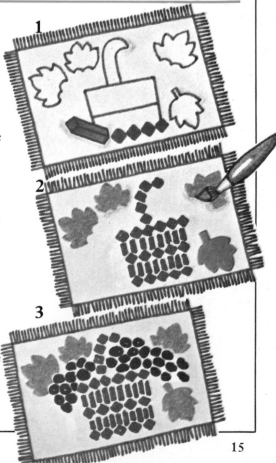

Pretty and practical hangers

Wooden coat-hangers can be padded with foam and covered in printed cloth to make them soft and attractive. They are ideal for hanging up 'best' clothes.

Cover coat-hangers in flowered patterns like the ones in the photograph. Or use bold, solid colours if you like.

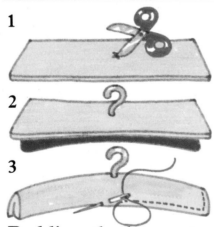

Padding the hanger

Measure and cut the strips of foam and cloth.
1. Make a tiny hole in the middle of the foam strip.
2. Push the hook of the hanger through the hole.
Fold the foam over the wood.
3. Sew the edges of the foam together with running stitch.

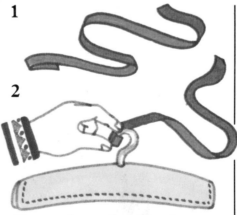

Covering the hook

If you wish to leave the hook uncovered, go on to step 1 of 'Making the cover'.
1. To cover the hook, fold over one end of the bias binding or binding cloth about 6mm.
2. Hold the folded end of the binding over the tip of the coat-hanger hook.

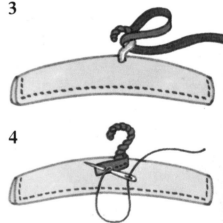

3. Wind the binding tightly round the folded end, then round and round the hook. Make the edges of the binding overlap each other.
Leave about 6mm of binding to spare and cut off any extra.
4. Back-stitch the end of the binding to the foam.

▶ You will need:
- ☐ Wooden coat-hanger, about 44cm long
- ☐ Strip of 6mm-thick foam rubber, 16cm × 48cm
- ☐ Printed cotton cloth, 20cm × 52cm
- ☐ Matching sewing cotton, pins
- ☐ Sewing needle, scissors
- ☐ Ruler or tape measure
- ☐ Ribbon, 30cm long for a bow
- ☐ Bias binding or strip of matching cotton cloth, 1cm × 40cm (optional)

Buy foam rubber from a hardware shop or large department store.

Try out the stitches on a spare piece of cloth first.

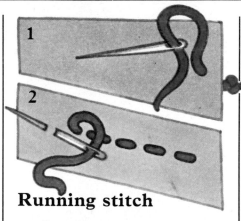

Running stitch

1. Push the needle and knotted cotton through the cloth.
2. Move the needle forward, then down and up through the cloth.
Make the stitches on the right side of the cloth the same length and the ones underneath half as long.

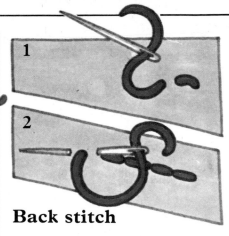

Back stitch

Push the needle through the cloth to the right side.
Move the needle backwards and push it down through the cloth.
1. Push the needle back up, in front of the first stitch.
2. Keep stitching in this way, putting the needle back into the hole of the last stitch.

Making the cover

Using the tip of the scissors, make a tiny hole in the middle of the piece of cloth.
1. Push the hook through the hole in the cloth.
2. Turn in the raw edges of the cloth about 1cm.
Using running stitch, hem the edges all round.

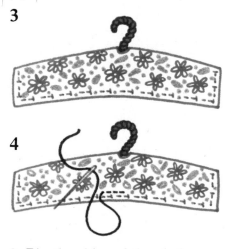

3. Pin the sides of the cloth together close to the edge.
4. Starting at the centre of the covering, make three or four small running stitches about 4mm from the edge.
Pull the stitches gently so that the cloth gathers slightly.

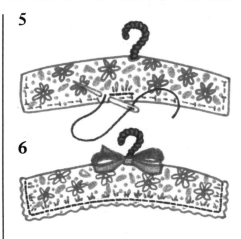

5. Now make a back stitch.
Repeat steps 4 and 5 until you have sewn the edges of the covering together.
Finish each section you sew with back stitch.
Remove the pins.
6. Tie the ribbon into a bow round the hook.

Pot-holders

Pot-holders are useful presents for adults who enjoy cooking. Try making the square one first as it's really quick and easy. Then make one glove or a pair of gloves, if you like.

Use washable cotton cloth for the covering and any thick washable cloth (such as towelling) for the padding. Make sure the padding *is* thick or the pot-holder will not be properly heat-proof.

1

22cm

Square pot-holder

▶ You will need:
- ☐ Cotton cloth, 22cm × 44cm
- ☐ Padding, 19cm × 38cm
- ☐ Tape or ribbon, 14cm long
- ☐ Sewing cotton, needle, pins
- ☐ Scissors, tape measure
- ☐ Pencil or dressmaker's chalk

1. Fold the cotton cloth in half, right sides facing.
Pin the open sides together.

2

3

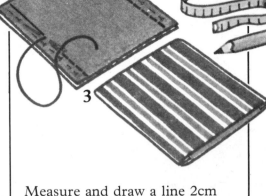

Measure and draw a line 2cm from the edge on both sides. This is the wrong side, so you can use chalk or pencil.
2. Back-stitch (see page 17) the two pinned sides along the lines you have drawn.
Leave the top edge open.
3. Remove the pins and turn the square right side out.

4   19cm

5

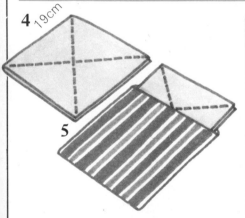

Fold the padding in half and pin the open edges together.
4. Back-stitch across the square from corner to corner.
Remove the pins.
5. Slip the padding inside the cotton square.

6

7

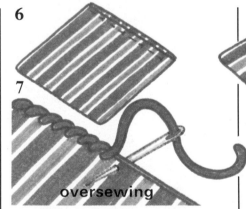

oversewing

Turn the raw edges of the cover 2cm to the inside.
6. Pin the open edges together. Oversew the edges but stop 3cm from the corner.
7. To oversew, work from the back of the cloth to the front, sewing close to the edge.

8

9

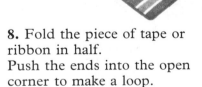

8. Fold the piece of tape or ribbon in half.
Push the ends into the open corner to make a loop.
9. Stitch the tape to the square by sewing through the tape and both layers of cloth.

Now try making a glove pot-holder as shown on the next two pages.

Glove pot-holder

▶ You will need:
- ☐ Cotton cloth, 28cm × 45cm
- ☐ Towelling for padding, 24cm × 80cm
- ☐ Tape or ribbon, 14cm long (optional)
- ☐ Sewing cotton, needle, pins
- ☐ Scissors
- ☐ Tracing paper, pencil and paper clips

Lay your tracing paper over the patterns and trace the smaller outline. Cut out the shape.
Trace and cut the larger pattern.
(Look at the 'Useful things to know' pages to help you.)

trace patterns

Use orange pattern for the cloth cover.

Use yellow pattern for the towelling padding.

1 2

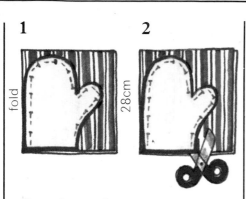

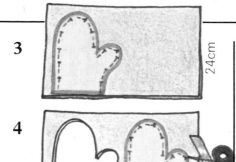

3 4

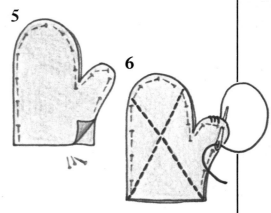

5 6

Cutting the cover

Fold the cotton cloth in half, wrong sides together.

1. Place the straight edge of the larger pattern on the folded edge of the cloth. Pin the pattern to the cloth through both layers.

2. Cut out the shape. Remove the pins.

Making the padding

Fold the towelling in half.

3. Pin the smaller pattern to it through both layers.
Cut round the paper pattern.
Remove the pins.

4. Pin the pattern to the spare towelling and cut another pair of hands.

5. Pin one pair of towelling hands together.

6. Back-stitch (see page 17) across each hand as shown, and oversew (see page 19) the top of the thumbs together.
Remove the pins.
Repeat steps 5 and 6 for the other pair of towelling hands.

Padding the glove

Open out the cloth glove, wrong side up.

7. Pin the towelling hands to the glove as shown. Back-stitch the towelling to the cotton cloth, but don't sew across the wrist edge. Remove the pins.
Fold the glove in half, right sides together.
Pin the glove edges together.

8. Back-stitch round the glove close to the towelling. Leave the wrist edge open.
Remove the pins.

9. Turn the wrist edge over 1cm.
Turn the wrist over another 1cm so that it meets the towelling.
Pin it into place.

10. Oversew the edges of cloth and towelling together.
Remove the pins.

7 8 9 10

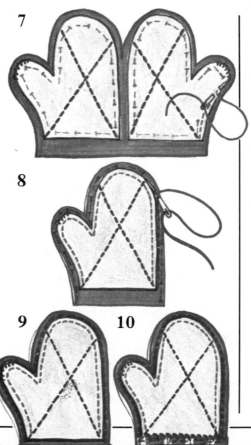

11

Adding a loop

To make a loop, fold the piece of tape or ribbon in half.

11. Pin the ends to the inside of the glove and oversew them to the towelling.
Remove the pins and turn the glove inside out.

Make another glove the same way if you want a pair.

Chipwood sun mobile

This jolly sun has been made from chipwood, or wood shavings.
Chipwood is very easy to use because it can be cut with scissors and glued together. Why not make the sun mobile for someone who wants to cheer up a room? You could make it in natural or coloured chipwood.

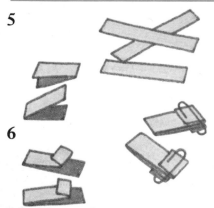

Making the rays

5. Gently bend each of the seven rays in half.
6. Carefully fold back the ends of the rays about 2cm to the outside.
Clip them together.

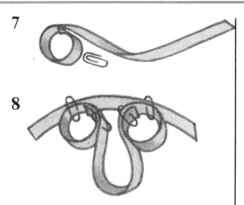

Making the face

7. Curl one end of the remaining long strip into a small circle to the inside.
Clip it into place.
Do the same at the other end.
8. Clip the eyebrow strip over the two eyes.
Leave the chipwood for a few hours to dry completely.

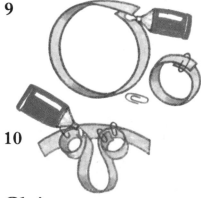

Gluing

Remove the clips from each piece first, and then use the glue sparingly.
9. Glue the ends of the big circle together and clip again.
Glue the ends of the small circle together and clip them.
Glue and clip the eyes.
10. Glue and clip the eyebrows.

You will need:

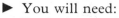

- ☐ Reel of natural or coloured chipwood, 2cm wide
- ☐ Bowl of water
- ☐ Tube of clear glue
- ☐ Twelve paper clips
- ☐ Pencil, ruler, scissors
- ☐ Needle, button thread
- ☐ Two weights to hold the chipwood flat
- ☐ Clean, dry cloth
- ☐ Two beads for the eyes, about 15mm in diameter
- ☐ One bead for the nose, about 2cm in diameter

You can buy chipwood and beads in a craft or hobby shop.

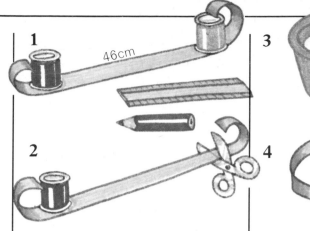

Weight the ends of the chipwood.

1. Measure and mark a strip 46cm long for the big circle.

2. Cut the strip.

Cut seven strips for the rays, each 18cm long.

Cut a strip 31cm long for the eyes and nose and one 15cm long for the eyebrows.

Cut an 8cm strip for a mouth.

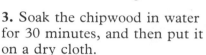

3. Soak the chipwood in water for 30 minutes, and then put it on a dry cloth.

4. Curl the longest piece into a circle. Overlap the ends slightly and hold them together with a paper clip.

Do the same with the shortest piece of chipwood.

11. Glue the flaps of one ray to the circle and clip them.

12. Remove one clip and glue the flap of another ray on to a flap of the first one.

Clip it into place again.

Glue on all the rays round the circle in the same way.

Let the glue dry, and then remove the clips.

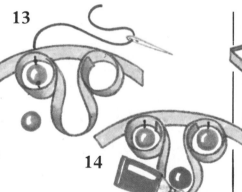

Adding the beads

Thread the needle with button thread, knotted at one end.

Slip an eye bead on to it.

13. Sew up through the eyebrow.

Knot and trim the thread.

Do the same for the other eye.

14. Glue the remaining bead into the nose and leave it dry.

Hanging the mobile

Knot a long piece of button thread and thread the needle.

15. Sew up through the top of the face. Make a knot and sew up through the circle.

16. Glue and clip the small mouth into place. Remove the clip when the glue is dry.

Hang up your mobile with the spare thread.

Coiled mats and holders

Rope is a very ordinary craft material, but you can coil and glue it into beautiful golden mats and containers. A flat circle is the easiest shape to make. With a little practice you can also coil rope into a bowl or a lidded holder. Make some mats for the family table. Or coil a holder for dad's paper clips or pencils.

▶ You will need:
☐ Tube of clear glue
☐ Pair of compasses
☐ Pencil, scissors
☐ Glass-headed pins
☐ Thick cardboard
  For the mat:
☐ 3 metres of rope
  For the holder:
☐ 7 metres of rope
☐ Glass bottle or jar about 19cm in diameter
  For the lid:
☐ 4 metres of rope

Choose sisal or hemp rope 6–8mm in diameter. Hemp is a smoother rope than sisal but it is more expensive. If you use sisal, wipe it with a wet cloth first to smooth the hairy bits. Buy either kind of rope from a craft or hobby shop.

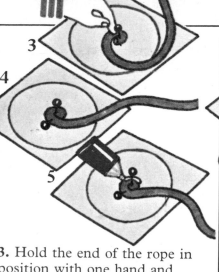

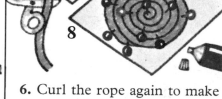

A round mat

Draw a circle with a 10cm radius on the cardboard. (Look at the 'Useful things to know' pages to help you.)

1. Push the pin through one end of the rope, and then push the pin into the centre of the cardboard circle.

2. Smear a little glue along the inside of the rope.

3. Hold the end of the rope in position with one hand and curl the spare rope anti-clockwise round the pin.

4. Pin through the rope to hold the first coil in place.

5. Smear glue along the outside of the first coil.

6. Curl the rope again to make the second coil.
Pin it into place as before.
Repeat steps 5 and 6 until the mat is the right size.

7. Cut off the spare rope at an angle.

8. Glue and pin down the end. Let the glue dry, then remove the pins.

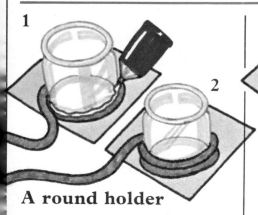

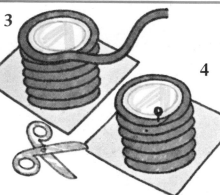

A round holder

Make a round mat one coil larger than the container.
Do not cut off the spare rope.
Let the glue dry and remove the pins.
Put the container on the mat.

1. Smear a little glue on the edge of the rope mat.

2. Coil the spare rope round the container once.

3. Keep gluing and coiling the rope until you reach the top of the container.
Cut off the spare rope.

4. Glue and pin the end of the rope to the last coil.
Leave the glue to dry.
Remove the glass container.

Making a lid

Follow step 1 of 'Try it first'.

1. Tie an overhand knot in the rope to make a knob.

2. Then follow the rest of the steps for 'A round mat'.

Now you can make mats, holders and lids any size you like. You will need more rope, of course, for bigger projects.

Knotted dog lead

Knotting is known as macramé (pronounced *mac-ra-may*). It is quick and easy to do. The dog lead has been made from dyed cotton string, but you could use ordinary parcel string. You can also do macramé with synthetic rope or cord. The thicker the cord, the more you will need for knotting.

▶ You will need:
For a 1 metre-long lead:
☐ 21 metres of string
☐ Dog collar clip
☐ Darning needle, scissors
☐ Ruler or tape measure

Hobby and craft shops sell all kinds of string. Buy the dog collar clip from a pet shop.

1

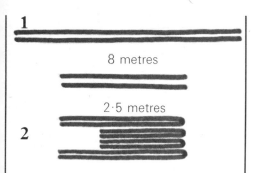

8 metres

2·5 metres

2

Preparing the string

1. Cut two pieces of string, each 8 metres long.
Cut two more pieces, each 2·5 metres long.
2. Fold each piece of string in half and lay the short lengths between the long ones.

Attaching the string

3. Put one of the long pieces through the ring of the clip.
4. Pass the ends through the loop and pull the knot tight.
5. Attach the two short lengths in the same way.
Then attach the other long piece of string.
You should now have four short lengths in the middle and two long ones on both sides.
The middle lengths are known as 'carrier cords'. The outer lengths are 'working cords'.
6. Hook the ring over something firm (such as a fixed nail or screw).
Sit on the carrier cords to keep them even and straight!

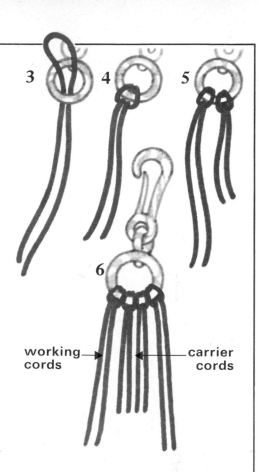

3   **4**   **5**

6

working→ cords   ←carrier cords

---

7   **8**

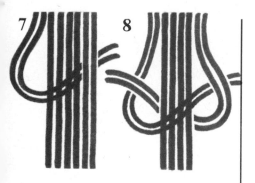

Making the knots

Take the two working cords on the left.
7. Pass them in front of the carrier cords, and then behind the working cords on the right.
Take the two working cords on the right.
8. Pass them behind the carrier cords, and then in front of the working cords on the left.
Pull the knot tight.

9

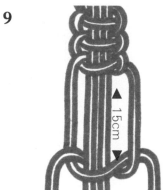

15cm

Repeat steps 7 and 8 a few times. When the lead begins to twist, use the working cords lying at the back as the left-hand cords.
Then continue knotting as before until the lead is 50cm long.
Leave about 15cm of string.
9. Begin knotting again, and continue until you have done another 30cm of knots.

10   **11**

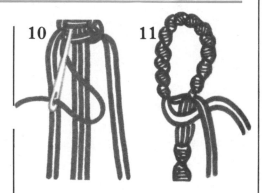

Knotting a handle

10. Thread the needle with one carrier cord and sew it back into the knots to conceal it.
Repeat step 10 with the three other carrier cords.
Loop the handle round.
11. Repeat steps 7 and 8 to finish knotting the spare cords.
Sew the working cords into the knots as shown in step 10.

► You will need:
□ Ball of parcel string, 3-5mm
  in diameter
□ Empty plant pot or potted
  plant and a spare pot
□ Sticky tape, scissors, ruler
□ Beads (optional)

Remember that the thicker the
string, the more you will need
for macramé. You could knot a
basket round an empty pot and
then plant something in it. Or
make a basket for a potted
plant by knotting round an
empty pot the same size.
If you want to use beads, make
sure the string will go through
the hole in the bead before you
buy them. To add beads, slip
them on the string before or
after you tie the knots.

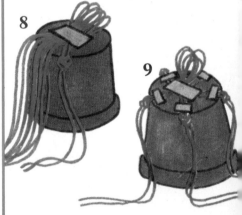

Macramé baskets

Flowers and plants look lovely
if you hang them up in baskets
of knotted string (or macramé).
Use parcel string to make an
economical present for mum.
Add beads if you like, but plain
baskets make attractive
presents, too.

8. Take two lengths of string
and make an overhand knot at
the edge of the base.
Tape this knot into position.
Repeat step 8 using two lengths
of string each time.
9. Tape each knot at roughly
equal distances round the base
of the pot.

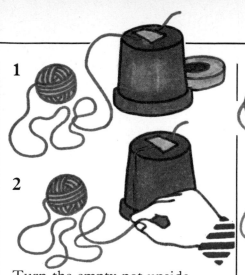

1

2

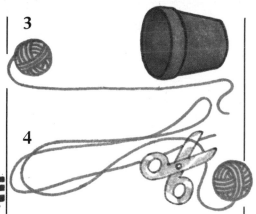

3

4

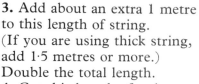

5

6

7

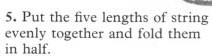

Turn the empty pot upside down.
Unwind a long piece of string from the ball.
1. Tape one end of the string to the centre of the base.
2. Drape the string over the edge of the pot to the rim. Hold the string at the rim and remove the sticky tape.

3. Add about an extra 1 metre to this length of string.
(If you are using thick string, add 1·5 metres or more.)
Double the total length.
4. Cut this length of string. Then using this piece as a guide, cut four more pieces of string all the same length.

5. Put the five lengths of string evenly together and fold them in half.
6. Tie an overhand knot about 10cm from the folded end.
7. Put the knot on the centre of the base of the pot and tape it into position.

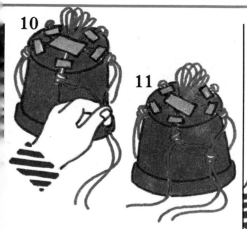

10

11

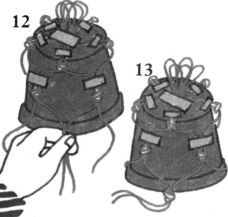

12

13

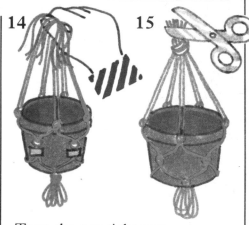

14

15

10. Hold together a length of string from each pair of knots.
11. Tie an overhand knot where the lengths of string meet.
Tape this knot into position.
Repeat steps 10 and 11 with all the lengths of string.
(Knot another row in the same way if your pot is very tall.)

For the next row of knots, take one length of string from each pair of knots again.
12. Hold the lengths together just above the rim of the pot.
13. Tie an overhand knot at the rim of the pot.
Repeat steps 12 and 13 with the other lengths of string.

Turn the pot right way up.
14. Pull all the lengths of string up together.
15. Tie an overhand knot near the top, and trim the ends of the string.
Remove all the sticky tape.
Your basket is ready to hang up on a hook or a pole.

Marzipan magic

Marzipan is a firm, sweet mixture of almonds and sugars which you can shape like plasticine. You can colour it with food dyes or leave it naturally yellow.

Why not make some of these tasty marzipan sweets for dad or for an uncle?

First ask mum if you can use her kitchen equipment.

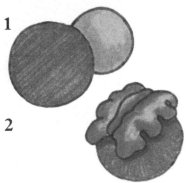

Nuts or dates

Use small pieces of plain or coloured marzipan.

1. To make nutty sweets, roll some marzipan into balls.

2. Press whole almonds or walnut halves into the balls.

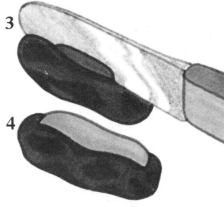

3. To make marzipan dates, slit the dates open with a knife and remove the stone.

4. Fill the centre of the date with an oblong of marzipan.

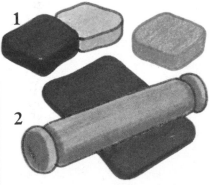

Catherine wheels

1. Divide half a packet of marzipan into three equal squares.

Colour each one differently.

2. Roll each piece into a flat oblong about 6mm thick.

▶ You will need:
- ☐ Packet of marzipan (or more, if you make all the sweets)
- ☐ Vegetable food dyes
- ☐ Cocoa powder
- ☐ Kitchen knife, rolling pin, wooden work board
- ☐ Walnuts or almonds, dates
- ☐ Caster sugar (optional)

Buy marzipan and vegetable food dyes in a supermarket. Once you have dyed the marzipan, it will keep for a week in an airtight tin. Before you begin, wash your hands and make sure that your work surface is clean.

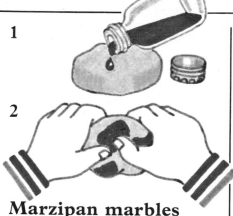

Marzipan marbles

Divide half a packet of marzipan into three equal pieces.
1. Drip a little vegetable dye on to one piece of marzipan.
2. Press and squash (or 'knead') the marzipan until the colour is evenly mixed in.
Dye the other two pieces with different colours.

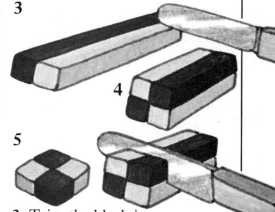

3. Push the three pieces of marzipan together.
Knead the marzipan gently to make a swirl of colours.
4. Break off small pieces and roll them into balls.

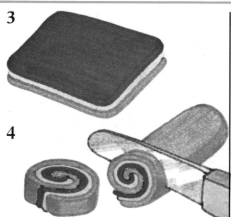

3. Lay the pieces on top of each other and press them firmly together to join them. Trim the edges with a knife.
4. Roll the marzipan up tightly and slice it into rounds.

Chequered marzipan

Break off two equal pieces of marzipan.
1. Sprinkle some cocoa powder on one piece and knead in the brown colouring.
Leave the other piece yellow.
2. Roll each piece into equal sausage shapes.
Put the sausage side by side and push them into a block.

3. Trim the block into an oblong.
Cut the oblong in half.
4. Put one half on top of the other to make alternate colours.
Push the two pieces together.
5. Cut the oblong into slices.

Frosting

Sprinkle caster sugar on the sweets if you like.

Sweet treats

Delicious things to eat are always popular as presents. Making frosty fruits or coconut ice is easy – and both are absolutely yummy!

Ask before you use mum's kitchen equipment.

▶ You will need:
  For the frosty fruits:
  ☐ Bunch of black grapes, some pears and red apples.
  ☐ 1 egg white, caster sugar
  ☐ Clean tea-towel, paintbrush
  ☐ Two sheets of waxed paper or foil about 30cm square
  ☐ Mixing bowl, fork

▶ You will need:
  For the coconut ice:
  ☐ 170g desiccated coconut
  ☐ 340g icing sugar
  ☐ 5 tbls condensed milk
  ☐ Cochineal colouring
  ☐ Sieve, pair of scales
  ☐ Mixing bowl, wooden spoon
  ☐ Wooden work board
  ☐ Plate, kitchen knife

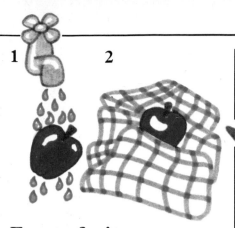

Frosty fruits

Wash your hands and make
sure that your work surface is
clean.
1. Wash all the fruits.
Leave the grapes in a bunch.
Gently dry the fruits with the
tea-towel.
2. Rub the apples and pears to
make them shiny.

3. Lightly beat the egg white
with a fork.
4. Sprinkle sugar on a sheet of
waxed paper or foil.
5. Dip the paintbrush in the
egg white and dab it over an
apple or pear.
You could paint all over the
fruit or make it streaky.

Now frost one fruit at a time.
6. Roll the fruit in the sugar.
Leave it to dry on the other
sheet of waxed paper or foil.
To frost the grapes, dab each
one with egg white.
7. Dip the bunch in sugar.
When the fruits are dry,
arrange them on a pretty dish.

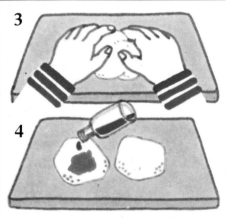

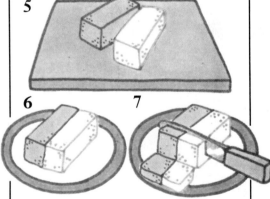

Coconut ice

Make sure that your hands and
the work board are clean.
Sieve the icing sugar into a
bowl.
1. Mix in the coconut.
Add the condensed milk.
2. Mix the ingredients together
with your hands.

3. Put the mixture on the
board and knead it until it is
smooth.
Divide it in half.
4. Drip a little cochineal on one
half of the mixture.
Knead the colour in until the
mixture is pink.

5. Shape the two halves of
coconut ice into oblongs.
Press the oblongs together.
Sprinkle a little icing sugar on
the plate.
6. Put the coconut ice on the
plate, and leave it for a few
hours until it is firm.
7. Slice the sweet into squares.

Glitter pouches

These heart-shaped felt pouches can be used in lots of different ways. Make them as holders for ribbons, hankies or tights. Or fill red felt pouches with sweets and hang them on the Christmas tree.
Use glue and glitter or sew on sequins and beads for a real film-star look.

▶ You will need:
For one pouch:
☐ 2 pieces felt, 20cm square
☐ Tube of clear glue
☐ 2 or 3 tubes of glitter in different colours
☐ Sequins or beads, sewing needle, cotton (all optional)
☐ Scissors or pinking shears
☐ Sewing needle, cotton, pins
☐ Dressmaker's chalk
☐ Tracing paper, pencil and paper clips

Using the pattern

Lay your tracing paper over the pattern and trace the outline.
(Look at the 'Useful things to know' pages to help you.)
Cut out the paper pattern.
Fold one piece of felt in half.
Put the straight edge of the pattern on the folded edge of the felt and pin them together.

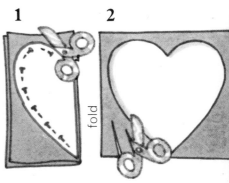

Making the felt heart

Make a zigzag edge by using pinking shears. Or use ordinary scissors for a smooth edge.
1. Cut round the paper pattern. Cut another felt heart in the same way.
2. Cut a straight strip from the scraps of felt if you want to make a loop for the pouch.

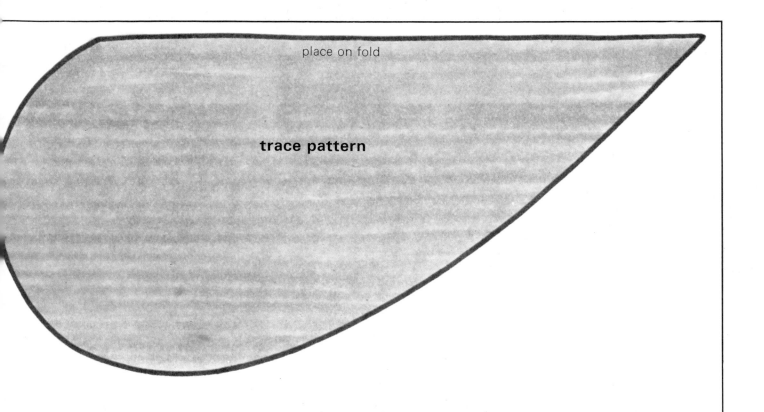

place on fold

trace pattern

3

4

Pin the two hearts together.
3. Leaving the top edge open, back-stitch (see page 17) through both layers of felt. Remove the pins.
4. To make the loop, glue one end of the felt strip to the back and the other end to the front of the heart.

Decorating the heart

Chalk your design on the heart.
5. Decide which lines to make one colour and trail a little glue along them.
6. Scatter glitter on the glue. Leave it to dry for at least ten minutes.
7. Shake off the extra glitter on to a piece of paper and pour it back into the tube.
Repeat steps 5–7 with the other colours.
8. Try making a pouch decorated with initials for a very individual present.
You could use glitter or sew on sequins and beads.

5

6

7

8

Felt badges

All the felt badges on this boy's jacket were made by his sister. No wonder he looks pleased! Felt shapes also make super presents for friends.
Make any of the badges you like, but always ask an adult before you attach them to someone's clothes.

▶ You will need:
☐ Scraps of coloured felt
☐ Scissors, pins
☐ Fabric glue or a sewing needle and cotton
☐ Tracing paper, pencil and paper clips

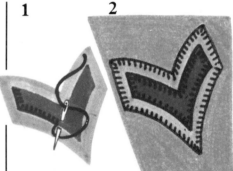

1 **2**

Sewn-on badges

For clothes that have to be dry-cleaned, you must sew on the badges.

Follow steps 1–3 as given for the 'Glued-on badges'.
1. Now sew the shapes together with blanket stitch.
2. Blanket-stitch the whole badge to the garment.

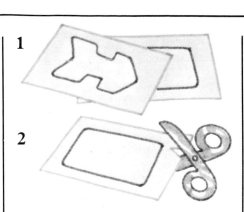

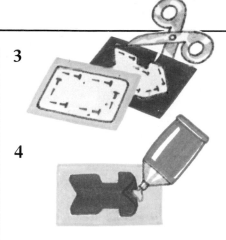

Glued-on badges

For washable garments such as denim jeans and jackets, you can make glued-on badges.

1. Trace the outer line of one of the patterns given below. Trace the inner lines on another sheet of paper. (Look at the 'Useful things to know' pages to help you.)
2. Cut out the paper patterns.

Pin the patterns to different-coloured pieces of felt.
3. Cut out the felt shapes. Remove the pins.
4. Carefully glue the smaller shape to the larger one. Glue the whole badge to the jacket or pair of jeans.

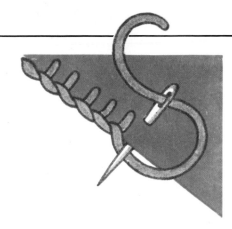

Blanket stitch

Thread the needle with cotton and knot the end.
Put the needle up through the felt. Make a loop with the cotton and put the needle back down into the felt.
Bring the needle out over the loop and pull it through.
Work from left to right, making stitches 4mm apart.

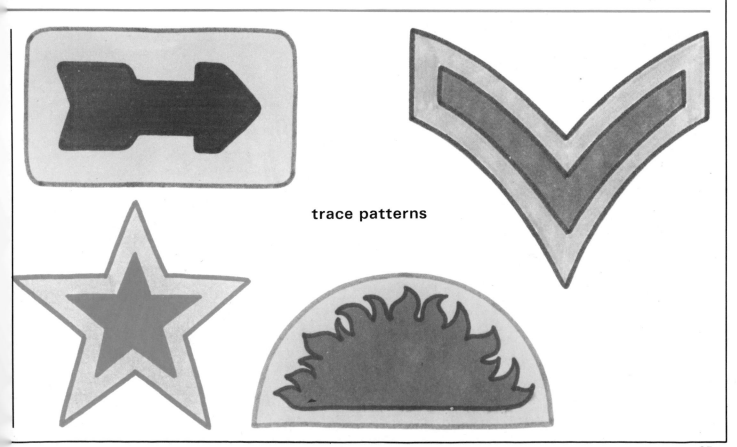

trace patterns

Now that you know how easy it is to use felt, try making some plump fruit 'jewelry'. You can make felt fruits that look good enough to eat! Give some to an older sister to pin to her favourite hat or sweater.

▶ You will need:
- ☐ Scraps of coloured felt
- ☐ Matching sewing cotton
- ☐ Sewing needle, scissors
- ☐ Cotton wool, pins
- ☐ Small safety-pins
- ☐ Tracing paper, pencil and paper clips

When you sew, use a double length of cotton in the needle.

Fruity felt 'jewelry'

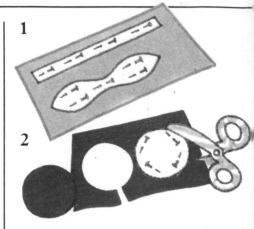

1

2

A pair of cherries

Make one trace pattern each for the stalk and leaves. Make two patterns for the cherry.
1. Pin the stalk and leaves patterns to green felt.
Cut out the shapes.
2. Pin the cherry patterns to red felt and cut two circles. Remove the pins.

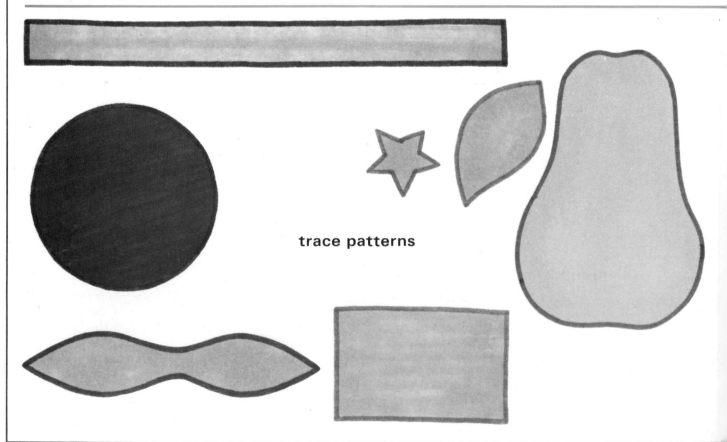

trace patterns

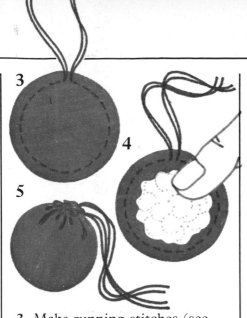

3. Make running stitches (see page 17) round one red circle. Leave long threads at each end.
4. Hold cotton wool on the felt.
5. Pull up the threads together and tie the ends tightly. Trim the spare thread. Repeat steps 3–5 with the other red circle.

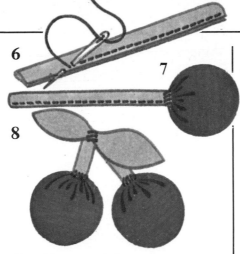

Stalks and leaves

Fold the cherry stalk in half, long sides together.
6. Back-stitch (see page 17) the edges together.
7. Oversew (see page 19) one cherry to each end of the stalk.
8. Fold the stalk in half and oversew the leaves to the bend.

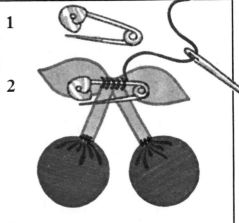

Fixing the pin

1. Open a safety-pin.
2. Sew it to the back of the felt fruits as shown.
Make sure you sew down the side of the pin which has the catch, and not the pointed side.

A juicy pear

Trace and cut out two pear shapes, two leaves, one star and one stalk.
You could make the pear in different shades of green felt.
Or use 'crazy' colours.

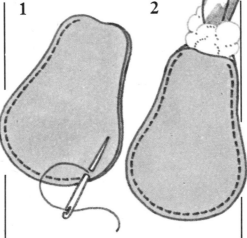

1. Back-stitch the two pear shapes together round the edges, leaving a gap at the top.
2. Using the point of the scissors, push cotton wool into the pear until it looks plump. Oversew the gap at the top.

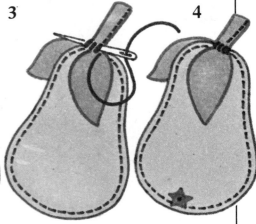

Fold the stalk in half and back-stitch the edges together.
3. Oversew the leaves and the stalk to the top of the pear.
4. Sew the star to the bottom. Sew on a pin as already shown.

Draw- string bags

Felt bags are marvellous presents because they can be used for so many things. Make them as soft shoe bags or as holders for cosmetics and hair brushes. You can make felt bags any size you wish. A boy would probably like a small one for his marbles or dominoes.

▶ You will need:
- ☐ 2 pieces of coloured felt, 30cm × 38cm
- ☐ 1·10 metres of 2·5cm-wide seam binding in a different colour
- ☐ A metre of cord to match the binding
- ☐ Sewing cotton the same colour as the felt
- ☐ Tape measure
- ☐ Sewing needle, pins
- ☐ Scissors, safety-pin

Buy seam binding and cord in the haberdashery department of a large store.

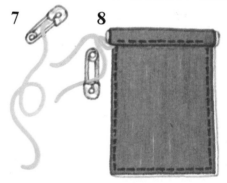

Threading the cord

Cut the cord in half.
7. Put the safety-pin through one end of one piece of cord.
8. Push the safety-pin and cord into one gap, along the channel, and out the same gap.

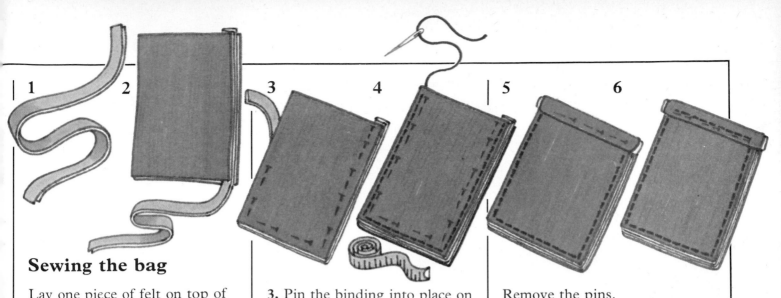

Sewing the bag

Lay one piece of felt on top of the other.
1. Fold the binding in half, long sides together.
2. Put the binding between the two layers of felt with the folded edge towards the middle of the bag.

3. Pin the binding into place on three sides.
The edge of the binding should be level with the edge of felt.
4. Back-stitch (see page 17) round the three sides about 4mm from the edge.
Sew through all layers of felt and binding.

Remove the pins.
5. Fold down the top of the bag 3cm and pin the edge.
6. Back-stitch along the folded edge 2cm from the top of the bag to make a channel for the cord.
Leave a 2cm gap in the stitching at each side seam.
Remove the pins.

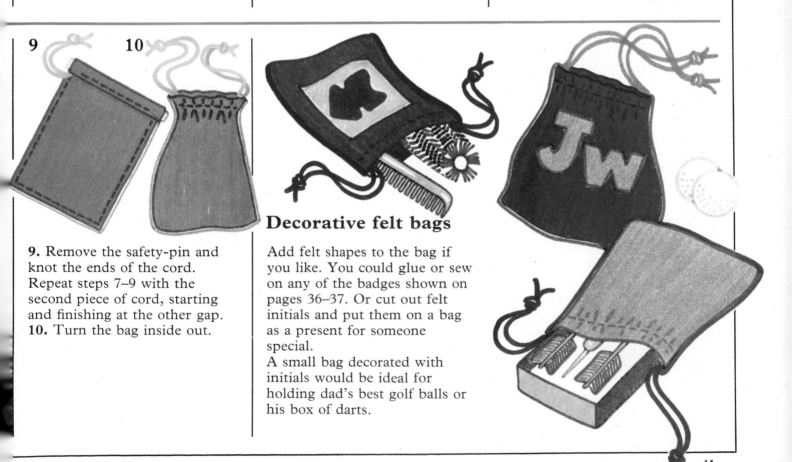

9. Remove the safety-pin and knot the ends of the cord. Repeat steps 7–9 with the second piece of cord, starting and finishing at the other gap.
10. Turn the bag inside out.

Decorative felt bags

Add felt shapes to the bag if you like. You could glue or sew on any of the badges shown on pages 36–37. Or cut out felt initials and put them on a bag as a present for someone special.
A small bag decorated with initials would be ideal for holding dad's best golf balls or his box of darts.

Wrapping it up

It always exciting to be given a beautifully wrapped present. Save up old boxes and put presents you have made in them. Wrap the boxes with paper, and decorate them with bows for a glamorous effect.

▶ You will need:
☐ Double-sided sticky tape
☐ Scissors
For the boxes:
☐ Square and round boxes
☐ Wrapping paper, pencil
For the bows:
☐ Two reels 16mm-wide ribbon in different colours

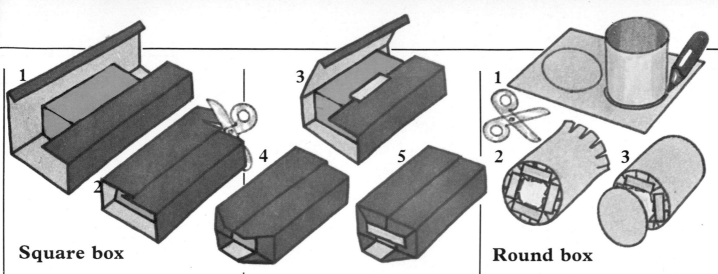

Square box

Cut a piece of wrapping paper that will completely cover the box. The paper should overlap at the top by about 5cm and extend well beyond the box ends.
Centre the paper under the box and wrap it round.
1. Trim the overlap and turn it under to make a neat edge.
2. Trim the ends to extend by half the depth of the box.

Tape the paper to the box top. (Look at the 'Useful things to know' pages to see how to use double-sided sticky tape.)
3. Press the overlap down.
4. Fold in the sides.
5. Turn down the top flap and tape across the folds.
Press up the bottom flap.
Do the same at the other end.

Round box

1. Draw round the top of the box on wrapping paper and cut out a circle.
Repeat step 1.
Wrap and trim the covering paper in the same way as shown for the square box.
2. Snip the ends of the paper and tape down the cut edges.
3. Press a circle on each end.

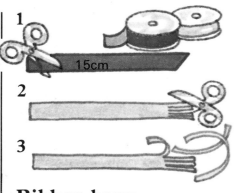

Ribbon bows

Cut a 15cm-length of ribbon.
1. Trim each end diagonally.
Cut the same length of ribbon in a different colour.
2. Snip the ends of this ribbon into a fringe.
3. Gently tear it along the cuts to make thin strips.

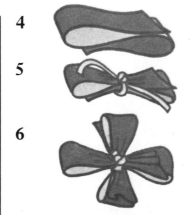

4. Loosely fold the wide piece of ribbon into an S-shape.
Try not to crease the ribbon.
5. Wrap one of the strips round the middle and knot it.
Don't knot too tightly.
Trim the ends of the knots.
Repeat steps 1–5 to make another bow.
6. Put one bow on the other.

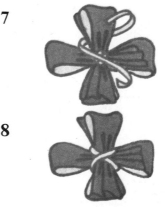

7. Curl a thin strip round the middle of the double bow.
Knot the strip behind.
8. The front of the bow should look like this.
Put sticky tape on the back and press the bow to the box.

If you look on pages 44–45 you will see lots more ideas for wrapping up presents.

Parcel decorations

The simplest ideas for decorating boxed presents are often the best. Why not wrap boxes with newspaper and decorate them with bands of shiny sticky tape? Or use brown tissue paper and tie it with sisal or string left over from a rope project.

You could also make an unusual gift box by wrapping it in contrasting papers.

Try snipping the ends of wrapping paper into a fringe. Or make frills as shown for the clowns on pages 10–11. You could decorate any boxed present with transfers, bunches of artificial flowers or gummed shapes and initials.